TRAVEL GUIDE

MARSEILLE

Your Passport to Adventure and Culture | The
Ultimate Guidebook to France's Mediterranean
Gem

Brian K. Kirby

Disclaimer:

The information provided in this book is intended for general informational purposes only. The author and publisher are not liable for any actions taken or decisions made based on the information contained in this book. Readers should consult with a professional for any specific advice or guidance related to their circumstances.

TABLE OF CONTENTS

CHAPTER 1: INTRODUCTION

Marseille, France's Mediterranean gem, awaits your discovery in "Travel Guide Marseille: Your Passport to Adventure and Culture" by Brian K. Kirby. In this introductory chapter, we will delve into the significance of this captivating destination and provide an overview of the exciting topics covered in this comprehensive travel guide.

Nestled along the picturesque coastline of the Mediterranean Sea, Marseille beckons with its rich history, vibrant culture, and breathtaking landscapes. As France's second-largest city, it is prominent in the country's tapestry of heritage and charm. Marseille's unique blend of Provençal traditions, Mediterranean influences, and North African flavors has shaped it into a captivating and diverse city that offers something for every traveler.

In "Travel Guide Marseille," we aim to be your trusted companion as you explore the wonders of this remarkable destination. This guidebook goes beyond surface tourist attractions, giving you a deeper understanding and appreciation of Marseille's hidden gems, local secrets, and off-the-beaten-path adventures.

Throughout the following pages, you will find a wealth of information to help you navigate the city and make the most of your time here. We will guide you through Marseille's captivating history, journeying from its ancient origins to its modern-day allure. You will discover the remarkable architectural landmarks that grace the cityscape, such as the awe-inspiring Basilique Notre-Dame de la Garde and the charmingly vibrant Vieux Port.

But Marseille is much more than its landmarks. It is a city alive with culture and creativity. We will lead you to the beating heart of Marseille's arts scene, where you can immerse yourself in world-class museums, vibrant street art, and the pulsating rhythm of music festivals. You will be able to witness the city's cultural fusion firsthand and embrace the lively atmosphere that pervades its streets.

Every exploration of Marseille would be complete with indulging in its culinary delights. Prepare to embark on a gastronomic journey, where you can savor the flavors of Provençal cuisine, from the iconic bouillabaisse to delectable street food and tantalizing pastries. Our curated dining recommendations will guide you to local eateries and hidden culinary treasures, ensuring that your taste buds are treated to an unforgettable experience.

For those seeking outdoor adventures, Marseille's natural beauty will leave you amazed. We will unveil the stunning Calanques, where towering limestone cliffs meet crystalline waters, inviting you to hike, swim, and marvel at their magnificence. The city's pristine beaches and scenic coastal trails offer endless opportunities to embrace the Mediterranean charm and indulge in relaxation and rejuvenation.

As you embark on your Marseille adventure, "Travel Guide Marseille: Your Passport to Adventure and Culture" will be your invaluable resource. We have carefully curated insider tips, practical advice, and detailed descriptions to help you confidently navigate the city and make the most of every moment.

So, pack your bags, open your mind to new experiences, and prepare to immerse yourself in the wonders of Marseille. Let this guidebook be your passport to adventure and culture as we embark on an unforgettable journey together. Get ready to uncover the secrets of Marseille, embrace its vibrant energy, and create memories that will last a lifetime. The captivating destination of Marseille awaits your exploration. Let's begin!

CHAPTER 2: GENERAL

INFORMATION

2.1 Location

Situated on the southeastern coast of France, Marseille is

nestled in Provence-Alpes-Côte d'Azur. This captivating

city overlooks the azure waters of the Mediterranean Sea, offering breathtaking views and a mild climate that attracts visitors from around the world.

2.2 Climate

Marseille enjoys a Mediterranean climate with hot, dry summers and mild, wet winters. Summers (June to August) are pleasantly warm, with temperatures ranging from 25°C - 30°C (77°F - 86°F), making it an ideal time to explore the city's outdoor attractions and relax on the beaches. Winters (December to February) are mild, with temperatures averaging around 10°C - 15°C (50°F - 59°F). Rainfall is spread throughout the year, but the wettest months are typically October and November.

2.3 Time Zone

Marseille operates on Central European Time (CET), which is UTC+1 during standard time and UTC+2 during daylight saving time. Adjusting your clocks accordingly when planning your itinerary or making travel arrangements is essential.

2.4 Currency

The official currency of Marseille and the rest of France is the Euro (EUR). ATMs are widely available throughout the city, and major credit cards are widely accepted. It is advisable to inform your bank of your travel plans to ensure uninterrupted access to your funds.

2.5 Entry Requirements

As a part of France, Marseille follows the entry requirements set by the Schengen Agreement. In order to gain entry into Marseille, individuals who hold citizenship in the European Union (EU) or the European Economic Area (EEA) must present a valid national identification card or passport. Citizens of other countries should consult their home country's French Embassy or Consulate to determine specific entry requirements. In most cases, a valid passport and, depending on your nationality, a visa may be required. Ensuring that your travel documents are valid for your stay is essential.

2.6 Specific Regulations

When visiting Marseille, it is important to familiarize yourself with any specific regulations or customs.

Here are a few points to note:

a) Health and Safety: Marseille is generally a safe city, but it is wise to take precautions to safeguard your belongings like any other urban area. Be aware of your surroundings and avoid displaying valuable items. It is also recommended to have travel insurance that covers medical expenses.

b) Local Customs: Marseille, like the rest of France, appreciates polite behavior and basic etiquette. Greeting people with a simple "Bonjour" (Good day) or "Bonsoir" (Good evening) goes a long way. It is customary to wait for the host to initiate the "la bise," the traditional cheek kiss, as a greeting. Dressing modestly, particularly when visiting religious sites, is also advised.

c) Language: The official language of Marseille is French. While English is spoken in tourist areas, learning a few basic French phrases to communicate with locals is helpful. Making an effort to speak French is often appreciated and can enhance your interactions and experiences.

2.7 Local Transportation

Marseille has a well-developed transportation network that allows visitors to navigate the city easily. The city offers extensive public transportation, including buses, trams, and a metro system. The Marseille-Provence Airport, located approximately 27 kilometers (17 miles) northwest of the city center, is the main air travel gateway. Taxis and car rental services are also available for those who prefer more flexibility in their transportation.

2.8 Emergency Services

In case of emergencies, Marseille has a reliable emergency service system. Remember to keep the emergency number 112 handy in case you need to contact the police, ambulance, or fire services. The phone number for your embassy or consulate should also be written down in case you want help while abroad.

By familiarizing yourself with these general details and adhering to the specific entry requirements, you can ensure a smooth and enjoyable visit to Marseille. As you embark on your adventure, prepare to immerse yourself in this magnificent Mediterranean gem's beauty, culture, and history.

CHAPTER 3: GETTING THERE

3.1 Flights

Marseille is well-connected to major cities worldwide, thanks to its international airport, Marseille-Provence Airport (MRS). Located approximately 27 kilometers (17 miles) northwest of the city center, this modern airport serves as the main gateway for air travel to Marseille. Numerous airlines operate regular flights to and from Marseille, offering a variety of domestic and international routes.

Travelers can find direct flights to Marseille from various European cities, including Paris, London, Barcelona, Rome, and Frankfurt. Connecting flights are available from farther destinations through major hubs such as Paris Charles de Gaulle Airport, Amsterdam Airport Schiphol, or Frankfurt Airport. You have a number of alternatives to choose from while entering or leaving the airport to make the process as easy as possible. Services for eating, shopping, and money exchange are among them.

3.2 Train Travel

Marseille is easily accessible by train, thanks to its well-developed rail network. The city boasts two major train stations: Marseille Saint-Charles and Marseille Blancarde. Marseille Saint-Charles is the primary station, serving both domestic and international routes. It is well-connected to various French cities, including Paris, Lyon, Nice, and Toulouse, as well as neighboring countries such as Spain and Italy.

France's high-speed train service, the TGV, offers efficient connections to Marseille from major French cities. For example, a TGV journey from Paris to Marseille takes approximately three hours, making it a convenient option for travelers from the capital.

3.3 Bus Travel

Traveling to Marseille by bus is an affordable and convenient option, especially for those coming from nearby cities or countries. The city is served by numerous bus companies, offering both domestic and international routes. The main bus terminal in Marseille is the Marseille Saint-Charles Bus Station, conveniently located near the Marseille Saint-Charles train station. From here, buses connect Marseille to destinations across France, including Paris, Lyon, Avignon, and Nice. International bus services connect Marseille to cities in neighboring countries, such as Barcelona, Geneva, and Milan.

3.4 Car Rentals

Car rentals are readily available in Marseille for travelers who prefer the flexibility of driving. Several major car rental companies have offices at Marseille-Provence Airport, allowing visitors to pick up and drop off their rental vehicles easily. Renting a car provides the freedom to explore Marseille and the stunning surrounding areas, including the picturesque Provence region and the scenic coastal towns along the French Riviera. It is important to note that driving in Marseille's city center can be challenging due to traffic congestion and limited parking options, so it is advisable to use public transportation or park in designated areas when exploring the city.

3.5 Local Transportation

Once you arrive in Marseille, getting around the city is a breeze, thanks to its efficient and diverse local transportation options.

3.5.1 Taxis

Taxis are available throughout Marseille and can be hailed on the street, found at designated taxi stands, or booked through taxi apps. Taxis are convenient for reaching specific destinations directly, especially if you have heavy luggage or prefer a door-to-door service. It is advisable to ensure that the taxi meter is activated at the beginning of your journey and to have some cash on hand for payment, although most taxis also accept credit cards.

3.5.2 Public Transit

Marseille boasts an extensive public transportation network consisting of buses, trams, and a metro system. Operated by Régie des Transports de Marseille (RTM), these modes of transport provide affordable and efficient ways to navigate the city.

- Buses: Marseille's bus network covers the entire city and its surrounding areas, offering an extensive network of routes. Bus stops are well-marked and can be found throughout the city, making reaching popular attractions and neighborhoods easy. The RTM website provides detailed bus route information, schedule, and fares.

- **Trams:** Marseille's tram network is a convenient mode of transportation, particularly for traveling within the city center. The trams connect various neighborhoods, major train stations, and tourist sites. They provide a comfortable and efficient way to explore Marseille's core areas.

- **Metro:** Marseille has two metro lines, M1 and M2, covering different city parts. The metro is fast and reliable for traveling longer distances or reaching destinations outside the city center. The metro operates from early morning until midnight, and tickets can be purchased at metro stations.

3.5.3 Rideshares

In Marseille, you can use ridesharing services like Uber and Bolt instead of traditional taxis. These services are accessible through mobile apps, which make it easy to request a ride and pay electronically. Ridesharing can come in handy for shorter trips or when you prefer the convenience of arranging transportation on your smartphone.

Marseille's transportation options cater to various preferences and budgets, allowing you to conveniently explore the city and its surroundings. Whether you fly, take a train or bus, rent a car, or rely on local transportation, your journey to and from Marseille promises to be seamless and enjoyable.

CHAPTER 4: ACCOMMODATION

When planning your trip to Marseille, finding the perfect accommodation is essential to ensure a comfortable and enjoyable stay. Marseille offers many options to suit every budget, preference, and travel style. In Marseille, there are various options for accommodations that cater to different tastes and budgets. Whether you prefer lavish hotels, snug guesthouses, or affordable hostels, there's something for everyone. Let's examine the various lodging options and offer suggestions to help you discover your perfect abode.

4.1 Hotels

Marseille boasts a diverse selection of hotels, ranging from high-end luxury establishments to boutique hotels and budget-friendly options. Hotels provide a comfortable and convenient stay, with private bathrooms, room service, and on-site dining options. They offer a range of room types, including single, double, twin, and family rooms. Many hotels in Marseille feature stunning views of the city, the Mediterranean Sea, or the Old Port.

Luxury Hotels: If you're seeking a luxurious experience, Marseille has a selection of five-star hotels that offer exquisite accommodations, exceptional service, and upscale amenities. These hotels often feature rooftop pools, spas, fine dining restaurants, and panoramic city or sea views.

Boutique Hotels: Marseille is known for its charming boutique hotels that provide a unique and intimate atmosphere. These hotels often have stylish interiors, personalized service, and a distinct character that reflects the city's cultural heritage.

Mid-range Hotels: For those seeking a comfortable stay without breaking the bank, mid-range hotels offer a balance between affordability and quality. These hotels provide well-appointed rooms, friendly service, and convenient locations near popular attractions.

Budget Hotels: Budget-friendly hotels are an excellent option for travelers seeking affordable accommodations in Marseille. These hotels typically offer basic amenities and comfortable rooms at a lower cost, making them ideal for budget-conscious travelers.

4.2 Guesthouses

Guesthouses, also known as bed and breakfasts or chambres d'hôtes, are popular for travelers seeking a more personalized experience. These accommodations are often privately owned and offer a cozy and intimate atmosphere. Guesthouses in Marseille range from traditional Provençal homes to modern apartments. They typically provide comfortable rooms, complimentary breakfast, and friendly hosts who can offer local tips and recommendations.

Guesthouses are ideal for travelers who appreciate a warm and welcoming environment, a personal touch, and the opportunity to interact with locals. They are often located in residential neighborhoods, allowing guests to experience the authentic local lifestyle.

4.3 Hostels

Hostels are an excellent choice for budget-conscious travelers or those seeking a sociable atmosphere. Marseille has several hostels that provide affordable dormitory-style accommodations and private rooms. Hostels often have common areas, communal kitchens, and organized activities that foster guest interaction.

Hostels are an excellent option for solo travelers, backpackers, or those looking to meet fellow travelers worldwide. They offer an opportunity to make new friends, share travel stories, and explore the city together.

4.4 Vacation Rentals

Vacation rentals, such as apartments, condos, and villas, offer a home-away-from-home experience in Marseille. These accommodations provide the convenience of having space and kitchen facilities and often include laundry facilities and Wi-Fi. Vacation rentals are available for short-term stays and can be an excellent option for families, groups, or those seeking more privacy and flexibility.

Platforms like Airbnb and HomeAway offer a wide range of vacation rental options in Marseille, allowing you to choose the size, location, and amenities that suit your needs.

4.5 Recommendations and Considerations

- **Location:** Consider the location of your accommodation based on your preferences and the attractions you plan to visit. The Vieux Port area is popular, offering easy access to Marseille's historic center, restaurants, and shopping. Neighborhoods like Le Panier, La Plaine, or the Prado area offer unique charms.

- **Budget:** Determine your budget and choose accommodations that fit within your financial constraints. It's important to keep in mind that prices can change based on the season. To ensure you get the best rates, it's recommended that you book in advance.

- **Amenities:** Consider the amenities important to you, such as Wi-Fi, air conditioning, breakfast, or on-site parking. Make a list of must-have amenities to help narrow down your options.

- **Reviews:** To understand the level of quality and service offered by accommodations, it's recommended to read reviews from past guests. Websites like TripAdvisor, Booking.com, and Google Reviews can provide valuable insights from fellow travelers.

- **Unique Considerations:** Marseille is a diverse and dynamic city, and different neighborhoods can offer distinct experiences. Consider whether you prefer to be in the heart of the bustling city center or a more tranquil area.

- **Booking Tips:** When booking accommodations, it's advisable to compare prices on different platforms, consider flexible cancellation policies, and check for special offers or discounts. Making reservations ahead of time is advisable, particularly during busy travel periods.

Remember to keep your preferences, budget, and travel style in mind when choosing your accommodation. Whether you opt for a luxurious hotel, a cozy guesthouse, a budget-friendly hostel, or a vacation rental, Marseille has various options to cater to your needs. Selecting the right accommodation will enhance your overall experience and provide a comfortable and convenient base to explore the city's adventure and culture.

CHAPTER 5: ATTRACTIONS AND ACTIVITIES

Marseille is a city that boasts a rich history, lively culture, and breathtaking natural landscapes. It provides a plethora of attractions and activities that cater to every traveler's interests. In this chapter, we will highlight Marseille's must-visit attractions and landmarks, providing detailed information about each site, its historical significance, and visiting hours. Additionally, we'll suggest popular activities that allow you to immerse yourself in Marseille's adventure and culture fully. Let's explore the wonders that await you!

5.1 Vieux Port (Old Port)

At the heart of Marseille lies the iconic Vieux Port, a bustling harbor that has been the city's center for trade and commerce for centuries. Stroll along the waterfront promenade, lined with colorful fishing boats, bustling cafes, and vibrant markets. Experience the lively atmosphere by witnessing the fishermen unloading their catch or indulge in a delectable seafood meal at any of the numerous waterfront eateries. The Vieux Port is the perfect place to soak in Marseille's maritime history and vibrant energy.

5.2 Basilique Notre-Dame de la Garde

Perched atop a hill overlooking Marseille, the Basilique Notre-Dame de la Garde is an iconic city symbol. This stunning Byzantine-style basilica, with its golden statue of the Virgin Mary, offers breathtaking panoramic views of Marseille and the Mediterranean Sea. Explore the ornate interiors adorned with mosaics and ex-votos, and marvel at the impressive architecture. The basilica holds deep cultural and religious significance for the people of Marseille and is a must-visit attraction for its historical and architectural beauty.

Visiting hours: The basilica is open daily, and visiting hours may vary. To ensure you have the latest information, it is recommended to check the official website.

5.3 Le Panier

Immerse yourself in Marseille's charming old town, Le Panier. This historic neighborhood, with its narrow winding streets, colorful facades, and lively atmosphere, offers a delightful glimpse into the city's past. Explore the local shops, boutiques, and art galleries that dot the streets, showcasing the creative spirit of Marseille. Don't miss visiting La Vieille Charité, an architectural masterpiece with a museum and cultural center.

Le Panier boasts several cafes, bars, and restaurants that offer a taste of Provençal cuisine. You can also unwind and take in the lively atmosphere while enjoying your meal.

5.4 Calanques National Park

The breathtaking beauty of the Calanques National Park will enchant nature enthusiasts. This stunning natural reserve boasts a series of deep limestone fjords, turquoise waters, and rugged cliffs. Hiking trails wind through the park, offering opportunities for exploration and adventure. Get ready to explore hidden beaches, soak in panoramic views, and experience the tranquility of this Mediterranean paradise by lacing up your hiking boots and embarking on a trek.

For those seeking a more leisurely experience, boat tours allow you to admire the Calanques' beauty from the water. Whether you hike, swim, or sail, a visit to the Calanques National Park promises unforgettable memories.

5.5 MuCEM (Museum of European and Mediterranean Civilizations)

Situated on the waterfront, the MuCEM is a contemporary museum that celebrates the cultural heritage of Europe and the Mediterranean region. Explore the thought-provoking exhibits that showcase Mediterranean civilizations' diverse histories, art, and traditions. The museum's architecture is a sight to behold, with its unique design blending modern elements with the historic Fort Saint-Jean. Take a leisurely walk across the footbridge connecting the MuCEM to Fort Saint-Jean and revel in the panoramic views of the city and the sea.

Visiting hours: The MuCEM is open daily, and visiting hours may vary. For the most reliable and up-to-date information, it is advisable to visit the official website.

5.6 Château d'If

Experience the world of Alexandre Dumas' renowned book, "The Count of Monte Cristo," by visiting Château d'If. This ancient fortress, situated on the island of If near Marseille, functioned as a penitentiary during the 16th and 17th centuries. Explore the cells, ramparts, and towers, and imagine the tales of the prisoners once held within its walls. The island's isolation and rugged beauty make it a captivating destination for history enthusiasts and literary fans.

Ferries operate regularly from the Vieux Port to Château d'If, providing convenient access to this historic landmark.

5.7 Cultural Experiences and Activities

Marseille's vibrant cultural scene offers many activities for those seeking immersive experiences.

Here are a few suggestions to enrich your journey:

- **Street Art Tour:** Embark on a guided tour of Marseille's vibrant street art scene, where talented local and international artists have transformed the city's walls into colorful masterpieces. Explore neighborhoods like Cours

Julien and La Belle de Mai to witness this dynamic expression.

- **Food Tours:** Delve into the culinary delights of Marseille with a guided food tour. Sample local specialties, such as bouillabaisse, pastis, and local cheeses, as you navigate the city's markets, bakeries, and cafes. Discover the secrets of Provençal cuisine and indulge in the flavors that define Marseille's gastronomic scene.

- **Boat Trips:** Take to the waters and embark on a boat trip along the Mediterranean coast. Enjoy the scenic views, visit nearby islands, or even go snorkeling or scuba diving to explore the rich marine life in these waters.

- **Music and Festivals:** Marseille is renowned for its lively music scene and vibrant festivals. Keep an eye out for music festivals, such as the Fiesta des Suds or the Marseille Jazz des Cinq Continents, where you can groove to diverse rhythms and melodies.

Consider joining guided tours or seeking local recommendations to immerse yourself in Marseille's cultural offerings fully and make the most of your time in this captivating city.

Marseille's attractions and activities encompass a rich blend of history, nature, culture, and adventure. Whether you explore iconic landmarks, wander through charming neighborhoods, hike the rugged Calanques, or indulge in the city's vibrant cultural experiences, Marseille promises a journey filled with unforgettable moments. Embrace the spirit of adventure and culture as you unravel the secrets of France's Mediterranean gem.

CHAPTER 6: DINING AND
ENTERTAINMENT

Marseille is not only a city of adventure and culture but also a gastronomic paradise. In this chapter, we will explore the vibrant dining scene of Marseille, from local restaurants and cafes to street food options. We'll delve into the city's rich culinary heritage, highlighting popular dishes and local specialties. Additionally, we'll provide information about the entertainment options available, including nightlife spots, theaters, music venues, and cultural events that add to Marseille's lively atmosphere. Prepare for a delightful culinary experience and enjoy the lively entertainment offerings of a stunning Mediterranean destination in France.

6.1 Dining in Marseille

Marseille's culinary scene is a delightful fusion of Mediterranean and Provençal flavors, showcasing fresh ingredients, aromatic herbs, and bold spices.

Here are some popular dining options to explore:

1. Traditional Provençal Cuisine: Marseille is known for its traditional Provençal dishes. Don't miss the opportunity to savor the iconic bouillabaisse, a flavorful fish stew made with a variety of local seafood, aromatic herbs, and saffron-infused broth. Pair it with a slice of rouille-slathered bread for the perfect combination. Other Provençal specialties include pissaladière (a caramelized onion and anchovy tart), panisse (chickpea flour fritters), and ratatouille (a vegetable stew).

2. Seafood Delights: As a coastal city, Marseille offers an abundance of fresh seafood. Indulge in oysters, mussels, clams, and prawns platters at one of the seafood restaurants lining the Vieux Port. Enjoy grilled fish such as loup (sea bass) or dorade (sea bream) drizzled with olive oil and sprinkled with aromatic herbs. The flavors of the Mediterranean come alive in every bite.

3. Mediterranean Influences: Marseille's cultural diversity is reflected in its cuisine. Explore the

Mediterranean influences that have shaped the city's culinary landscape. Sample dishes such as couscous, kebabs, and falafel from the vibrant neighborhood of Noailles, home to a large North African community. These flavors will transport you to the bustling souks and lively streets of the Mediterranean.

4. Street Food Delights: Marseille is known for its vibrant street food scene, offering quick and delicious bites that reflect the city's multiculturalism. Try the famous panisses, crispy chickpea flour fritters served hot, or the irresistible socca, a thin chickpea pancake. Visit local markets, such as Marché des Capucins or Marché Noailles, to experience the diverse range of street food options available.

6.2 Dietary Considerations

Marseille's dining scene caters to various dietary preferences and restrictions. Many restaurants provide vegetarian and vegan options that showcase the region's abundant produce through innovative dishes. When dining out, informing the waitstaff about any dietary restrictions or allergies is helpful to ensure that your needs are accommodated. Additionally, gluten-free options are becoming more prevalent in Marseille, with several establishments offering gluten-free alternatives. Exploring the city's culinary landscape can delight all, regardless of dietary considerations.

6.3 Entertainment in Marseille

Beyond its culinary delights, Marseille offers a vibrant entertainment scene that will captivate visitors.

Here are some recommendations for a memorable evening in the city:

1. Nightlife Spots: Marseille's nightlife is diverse and dynamic, offering something for everyone. Head to the vibrant Cours Julien neighborhood, known for its trendy bars and live music venues. Explore the buzzing nightlife around La Plaine, where you can find a mix of bars, clubs, and outdoor terraces. The Vieux Port area also comes alive at night, with waterfront bars and lounges offering spectacular views and a relaxed atmosphere.

2. Theaters and Performing Arts: Marseille boasts a thriving theater scene, with numerous venues showcasing a range of performances, from traditional plays to experimental productions. Check out the Théâtre de la Criée or the Théâtre Toursky for a dose of cultural enrichment. The Opéra de Marseille is another iconic venue hosting opera, ballet, and classical performances.

3. Music Venues: Marseille's music scene is vibrant and diverse, encompassing a range of genres and styles. Experience live music at venues like Le Moulin, known for its eclectic programming, or Espace Julien, a popular concert hall hosting local and international acts. From jazz and rock to world music and electronic beats, there's always something to suit your musical taste.

4. Cultural Events: Marseille is known for its cultural events celebrating art, music, and local traditions. Keep an eye out for festivals such as Marseille Jazz des Cinq Continents, where world-renowned jazz musicians gather to perform in various venues across the city. The Fiesta des Suds is another highlight, featuring a mix of music genres and cultural festivities.

Immerse yourself in Marseille's vibrant entertainment scene, attend cultural events, and discover local venues that showcase the city's artistic and musical talents. The lively atmosphere and diverse offerings will make your evenings in Marseille memorable as your daytime adventures.

As you explore the dining and entertainment options in Marseille, allow yourself to be enchanted by this captivating Mediterranean city's flavors, sounds, and vibrant energy. Whether indulging in traditional Provençal cuisine, savoring street food delights, or immersing yourself in the city's lively nightlife, Marseille promises to satisfy your appetite for adventure and culture.

CHAPTER 7: SHOPPING AND

SOUVENIRS

Marseille offers a vibrant shopping scene that combines traditional markets, trendy boutiques, and bustling shopping districts. In this chapter, we will explore the city's popular shopping destinations, recommend unique local products and handicrafts, and provide tips for making the most of your shopping experience. Whether you're searching for fashion, local delicacies, or souvenirs to commemorate your visit, Marseille has something to suit every taste and budget.

7.1 Popular Shopping Districts

1. Rue Saint-Ferréol: In the heart of Marseille, Rue Saint-Ferréol is a bustling pedestrian street with shops and boutiques. Here, you'll find well-known international brands, popular department stores like Galeries Lafayette, and local retailers offering fashion, accessories, cosmetics, and more.

2. Cours Julien: If you're searching for a more bohemian and artistic atmosphere, head to Cours Julien. This vibrant neighborhood is known for its independent boutiques, vintage stores, art galleries, and street art. It's the perfect place to find unique and one-of-a-kind items, including clothing, accessories, and artwork.

3. La Rue Paradis: La Rue Paradis is Marseille's luxury shopping destination, featuring high-end fashion boutiques and designer stores. This elegant street showcases renowned brands and offers a sophisticated shopping experience for fashion enthusiasts.

4. Les Terrasses du Port: For a modern shopping experience, visit Les Terrasses du Port. This contemporary shopping center is located near the waterfront. The shopping center offers a diverse selection of local and global brands and several dining choices. Additionally, a rooftop terrace boasts breathtaking views of the city and the Mediterranean Sea.

7.2 Markets

1. Le Marché aux Puces de Marseille: Known as the flea market of Marseille, Le Marché aux Puces is a treasure trove for antique lovers and bargain hunters. This sprawling market offers various vintage items, including furniture, clothing, jewelry, and unique collectibles. Spend a leisurely day exploring the market's stalls and uncovering hidden gems.

2. Marché de la Joliette: Located near the Vieux Port, Marché de la Joliette is a lively market where locals gather to shop for fresh produce, regional specialties, and artisanal products. The market showcases Provence's vibrant flavors and colors, offering an opportunity to immerse yourself in the local culinary scene.

3. Marché Noailles: For an authentic taste of Marseille's multiculturalism, visit Marché Noailles. This bustling market is a melting pot of flavors, featuring a diverse range of products worldwide. Explore the spice stalls, browse through exotic fruits and vegetables, and discover a variety of international ingredients and delicacies.

7.3 Unique Local Products and Souvenirs

Marseille is known for its unique local products and handicrafts that make for memorable souvenirs.

Here are some recommendations:

1. Savon de Marseille: A visit to Marseille is complete with picking up a bar of Savon de Marseille. This traditional soap is made from vegetable oils and dates back centuries. Look for authentic Savon de Marseille stamped with the official logo, and choose from various scents and sizes.

2. Culinary Delights: Marseille's culinary heritage offers an array of edible souvenirs. Consider purchasing a bottle of local olive oil, flavored salts, or herbs de Provence, a blend of aromatic herbs traditionally used in Provençal cooking. Other popular food items include calisson d'Aix (a sweet almond paste treat) and navettes (boat-shaped cookies).

3. Local Art and Crafts: Marseille is a hub of creativity and artistic expression. Support local artists by purchasing unique artworks, ceramics, or jewelry from boutiques and galleries in neighborhoods like Le Panier and Cours Julien. Look out for pieces that capture the spirit of Marseille and its vibrant cultural scene.

4. Traditional Provençal Fabrics: Provençal fabrics are renowned for their lively hues and unique designs, making them delightful mementos. Look for items made from traditional Provençal fabrics, such as tablecloths, tea towels, or tote bags adorned with sunflowers, olive branches, or cicadas motifs.

7.4 Shopping Tips

- **Bargaining:** Bargaining is not widely practiced in Marseille's retail shops or markets. However, if you come across an antique shop or a flea market stall, there may be room for negotiation. It's always best to approach bargaining with respect and a friendly attitude.

- **VAT Refund:** Non-European Union (EU) residents may be eligible for a Value Added Tax (VAT) refund on certain purchases. Look for shops displaying the "Tax-Free Shopping" logo and request a tax refund form. Remember to keep your receipts and present the necessary documentation at the airport when departing the EU to claim your refund.

- **Opening Hours:** Most shops in Marseille are open from Monday to Saturday, with some smaller establishments closing for a few hours in the afternoon. More extensive shopping centers and department stores often have extended hours and are open on Sundays.

- **Payment Options:** Major credit cards are widely accepted in most shops and boutiques. However, it is always advisable to carry some cash, especially when shopping in smaller markets or at local vendors.

- **Authenticity and Quality:** When purchasing local products or handicrafts, look for authentic labels or indications of quality. Ask the shopkeeper or vendor about the origin and production methods to ensure you're buying genuine, locally-made items.

Exploring Marseille's shopping scene allows you to discover unique treasures and take a piece of the city's charm back home. From trendy boutiques to vibrant markets, the options are diverse and exciting. Remember to savor the experience, immerse yourself in the local culture, and indulge in the delights Marseille's shopping and souvenirs offer.

CHAPTER 8: SAFETY AND HEALTH

When traveling to Marseille, it's essential to prioritize your safety and health to ensure a smooth and worry-free journey. In this chapter, we will provide general safety tips, offer advice on protecting your personal belongings, discuss common scams to be aware of, and highlight local customs to respect. We will also provide information on the destination's emergency services, hospitals, and medical facilities. Additionally, we'll address any specific health risks, required vaccinations, or necessary precautions you should take while visiting Marseille.

8.1 General Safety Tips

Marseille is a safe city overall, but taking precautions to ensure your well-being during your trip is always wise.

Here are some general safety tips to keep in mind:

1. Be Mindful of Your Belongings: Like any popular tourist destination, Marseille has its share of petty theft. Keep your belongings secure, and be cautious in crowded areas, public transportation, and tourist hotspots. It is advisable to refrain from carrying a large sum of cash or valuable items while traveling. Instead, utilize hotel safes or secure locks to safeguard your belongings.

2. Stay Aware of Your Surroundings: It's important to be aware and alert to your surroundings, especially when you are in an unfamiliar place. Avoid isolated or poorly lit streets at night, and trust your instincts if a situation seems suspicious. Traveling in groups or with a companion can enhance safety, particularly during nighttime outings.

3. Dress Appropriately: While Marseille is a diverse and multicultural city, it is important to be mindful of local customs and dress respectfully when visiting religious sites or conservative areas. This includes covering your shoulders, avoiding short skirts or shorts, and removing your shoes if required.

4. Follow Local Laws and Customs: Familiarize yourself with local laws and customs to avoid inadvertent violations. For example, it is illegal to drink alcohol in public areas unless in designated places or during specific events. Respect local customs, traditions, and religious practices, particularly in places of worship.

5. Use Reliable Transportation: Opt for official taxis, reputable ridesharing services, or public transportation when getting around the city. It's important to be careful when choosing taxis and to ensure they are licensed. Always double-check the fare with the driver before beginning your trip.

6. Stay Connected: Ensure you have a reliable means of communication, such as a working mobile phone with programmed emergency contacts or a local SIM card for easy access to local services. Inform a trusted person about your travel plans and regularly check in with them during your trip.

8.2 Protecting Your Health

Regarding health, it's important to take certain precautions to ensure a safe and healthy journey in Marseille.

Here are some considerations:

1. **Medical Insurance:** Before traveling, ensure comprehensive travel medical insurance covering emergency medical expenses, including hospitalization and medical evacuation.

2. **Vaccinations:** Check with your healthcare provider or travel clinic to ensure you are current on routine vaccinations. They may also advise additional vaccinations based on your travel plans and personal health history. Commonly recommended vaccinations for France include Tetanus, Diphtheria, Pertussis, Measles, Mumps, Rubella, and Influenza.

3. Sun Protection: Marseille enjoys a Mediterranean climate with plenty of sunshine. Protect yourself from the sun's harmful rays by using sunscreen with a high SPF, wearing protective clothing, and wearing sunglasses and a hat.

4. Hygiene Precautions: Maintaining good hygiene practices by regularly washing your hands with soap and water is important. If soap is unavailable, hand sanitizer can be used as an alternative. Avoid consuming tap water and opt for bottled water instead.

5. Traveler's Diarrhea: To avoid traveler's diarrhea, which can result from consuming contaminated food or water, take precautions such as drinking bottled or purified water, avoiding raw or undercooked food, and practicing good hand hygiene.

8.3 Emergency Services and Medical Facilities

Marseille has a well-developed emergency service system, and help is readily available.

Here's what you should know:

1. Emergency Numbers: In case of an emergency, dial the European emergency number 112 for assistance. This number can be used for police, fire, or medical emergencies.

2. Hospitals and Medical Facilities: Marseille has several hospitals and medical facilities that provide comprehensive healthcare services. Some well-known hospitals in Marseille include Hôpital de la Timone, Hôpital Nord, and Hôpital Européen Marseille. These hospitals have emergency departments and can handle a range of medical conditions.

3. Pharmacies: Pharmacies, known as "Pharmacies de Garde," are available throughout the city. They provide over-the-counter medications and can offer advice on minor ailments. Note that pharmacies in Marseille may have different opening hours, so it's advisable to check for the nearest open pharmacy if you need urgent medication or assistance outside regular hours.

4. Medical Assistance for Travelers: If you require medical assistance specifically for travelers, such as travel vaccinations or travel health advice, consider visiting a travel health clinic before your trip. Personalized recommendations tailored to your travel plans and health history can be provided.

It's essential to have travel insurance that covers medical emergencies, as medical treatments can be costly for non-residents. Keep a copy of your insurance policy and emergency contact information readily accessible during your trip.

8.4 Specific Health Risks and Precautions

Marseille does not have any specific health risks that are unique to the city. However, staying informed about current health advisories or disease outbreaks is always advisable before your trip.

Here are some general health precautions to consider:

1. Mosquito-Borne Diseases: While Marseille does not have a high risk of mosquito-borne diseases, protecting yourself from mosquito bites is still advisable, particularly during the warmer months. To avoid mosquito bites, it is recommended to apply insect repellent, wear clothing that covers your arms and legs, and sleep in rooms that have air-conditioning or mosquito nets as needed.

2. COVID-19 Precautions: As of the time of writing, the COVID-19 pandemic is ongoing. Stay updated on travel advisories, follow local guidelines and regulations, and adhere to recommended preventive measures such as wearing masks, practicing physical distancing, and maintaining good hand hygiene.

It's always a good idea to consult your healthcare provider or a travel medicine specialist before traveling to Marseille. Personalized advice can be provided based on your medical history, current health status, and travel plans.

By following these safety and health guidelines, you can ensure a secure and enjoyable experience in Marseille.

CHAPTER 9: LOCAL TRANSPORTATION

Getting around Marseille is a breeze, thanks to its well-connected transportation system. This chapter will provide you with essential information about the local transportation options in Marseille. From subway and bus routes to fares and schedules, we'll ensure you have all the details to navigate the city easily. We'll also explore alternative transportation options, such as renting bicycles and scooters, for a more adventurous way to explore Marseille's streets.

9.1 Subway and Bus System

The public transportation system in Marseille consists of a subway (known as the Métro) and an extensive bus network.

Here's what you need to know about each mode of transport:

1. Métro:

The Marseille Métro is a convenient and efficient way to travel within the city. It consists of two subway lines, Line 1 (blue) and Line 2 (red), which cover most of the main areas and attractions.

- **Line 1:** Line 1 runs from La Rose to La Fourragère, connecting major hubs such as Vieux Port, Gare Saint-Charles (the main train station), and Castellane.

- **Line 2:** Line 2 runs from Bougainville to Sainte-Marguerite-Dromel, passing through important stops like Joliette, Vieux Port, and Rond-Point du Prado.

The subway operates from around 5:00 am until midnight, with trains running approximately every 5 to 10 minutes during peak hours and every 10 to 15 minutes during off-peak times. The frequency may vary on weekends and public holidays, so it's advisable to check the official transportation website or consult the station timetables for the most up-to-date information.

2. Bus:

The bus network in Marseille is extensive and covers the entire city, including the outskirts and nearby towns. Buses are an excellent option for reaching destinations not served by the subway or exploring areas off the beaten path.

The bus routes are numbered, and each bus stop is marked with route maps and timetables. Bus schedules differ based on the route and time of day, with more frequent service provided during peak hours. Buses typically operate from early morning until around 9:00 pm, although some routes have extended service until later. Night buses (Noctambus) are available for late-night travel.

Fares for the subway and bus system are integrated, and tickets can be used interchangeably within a specified time frame. Tickets can be bought from vending machines situated at subway stations or from the bus driver directly.

It's important to validate your ticket upon boarding the bus or entering the subway platforms to avoid penalties.

For more detailed information about subway and bus routes, fares, and schedules, refer to the official transportation website or pick up a local transportation map available at subway stations, tourist information centers, or from the bus driver.

9.2 Alternative Transportation Options

In addition to the subway and bus system, Marseille offers various alternative transportation options that allow you to explore the city at your own pace.

Here are a few popular options:

1. Bicycle Rentals:

Marseille has a bike-sharing program called "Le vélo" that allows you to rent bicycles for short trips. You can find bike stations throughout the city, and the rental process is simple and convenient. Download the bike-sharing app, register, and locate the nearest bike station. Once at the station, follow the instructions to unlock a bike using the app. Enjoy cruising through Marseille's streets and return the bike to any bike station when finished.

2. Scooter Rentals:

Electric scooters have gained popularity in Marseille as a fun and efficient mode of transportation. Several companies offer scooter rentals through smartphone apps. Download the app, sign up, locate a nearby scooter, and unlock it using the app. Remember to adhere to traffic rules and wear a helmet for your safety.

3. Walking:

Marseille's compact city center and charming neighborhoods make it ideal for exploring on foot. Many of the city's attractions, including the Vieux Port, Le Panier, and the MuCEM, are within walking distance of each other. Strolling through the city allows you to discover hidden gems, enjoy the local atmosphere, and appreciate Marseille's architectural beauty up close.

4. Taxis and Ridesharing:

Taxis are readily available throughout Marseille, and you can easily hail them on the street or find them at designated taxi stands. Alternatively, you can use popular ridesharing services like Uber or Lyft, which operate in the city. These services provide a convenient and reliable way to get around, particularly if traveling in a group or having specific transportation needs.

When using alternative transportation options, be mindful of local traffic regulations, respect pedestrian areas, and park scooters and bicycles in designated parking zones to avoid fines.

9.3 Accessibility Considerations

Marseille's transportation system is designed to accommodate people with mobility challenges. The subway stations have elevators or escalators for easier access, and many buses have ramps for wheelchair accessibility. However, you should check the official transportation website for specific accessibility information or contact the transportation authorities for special assistance.

9.4 Useful Tips for Using Local Transportation

- **Get a Transportation Pass:** If you plan to use public transportation frequently during your stay in Marseille, consider purchasing a transportation pass. The Pass Navigo is a rechargeable card that offers unlimited rides within a specified duration. It provides convenience and cost savings compared to purchasing individual tickets.

- **Plan Your Routes:** Before starting your journey, familiarize yourself with the subway and bus routes to determine the most efficient way to reach your destination. Use online journey planners, mobile apps, or consult transportation maps to help you navigate the city's public transportation system effectively.

- **Be Mindful of Rush Hour:** Like any major city, Marseille experiences peak hours when the subway and buses can be more crowded. Plan your travel outside these times to avoid the crowds and ensure a more comfortable journey.

- **Keep Valuables Secure:** Be vigilant about your personal belongings while using public transportation. Keep your bags close to you and be aware of your surroundings to deter any potential pickpockets.

- **Stay Updated:** Public transportation schedules may occasionally change due to maintenance or special events. Stay updated by checking the official transportation website, following social media accounts for updates, or using mobile apps that provide real-time information on transit schedules and delays.

Marseille's local transportation system offers convenient and efficient options for getting around the city. Whether you navigate the subway and bus network, rent a bicycle or scooter, or explore on foot, you'll find that Marseille is easily accessible and well-connected. Experience the joy of wandering through the city at your own leisure and embrace the excitement ahead at every turn.

CHAPTER 10: LANGUAGE AND COMMUNICATION

Knowing the local language and communication options can significantly enhance your travel experience when visiting Marseille. This chapter will provide basic language phrases, translations, and pronunciation guides to help you navigate daily interactions with locals. We will also cover information on mobile network coverage, SIM card availability, and internet access to stay connected during your adventures in France's Mediterranean gem.

10.1 Language Basics

The official language spoken in Marseille is French. While many locals understand and can communicate in English, especially in tourist areas, it's always appreciated when visitors try to speak a few basic French phrases.

Here are some essential phrases and translations to help you communicate effectively:

1. Greetings and Basic Phrases:

- Hello: Bonjour (bohn-zhoor)

- Goodbye: Au revoir (oh ruh-vwar)

- Please: S'il vous plaît (see voo play)

- Thank you: Merci (mehr-see)

- You're welcome: De rien (duh ree-ehn)

- Excuse me: Excusez-moi (ex-koo-zay mwa)

- Yes: Oui (wee)

- No: Non (nohn)

2. Introductions:

- My name is...: Je m'appelle... (zhuh mah-pehl)

- What is your name?: Comment vous appelez-vous? (kom-mohn vooz ah-puh-leh voo?)

- Nice to meet you: Enchanté(e) (ahn-shahn-tey)

3. Asking for Help:

- Could you assist me, please?Could you assist me, please??: Pouvez-vous m'aider, s'il vous plaît? (poo-vey voo may-day, see voo play?)

- I don't understand: Je ne comprends pas (zhuh nuh kohm-prahn pah)

- I need help: J'ai besoin d'aide (zhay buh-zwahn dehd)

4. Ordering Food and Drinks:

- I would like...: Je voudrais... (zhuh voo-dreh)

- The bill, please: L'addition, s'il vous plaît (lah-dee-syohn, see voo play)

- Cheers!: Santé! (sahn-tay)

Remember to approach conversations with a friendly and respectful attitude, and locals will appreciate your efforts to communicate in their language.

10.2 Mobile Network Coverage and SIM Cards

Staying connected while traveling in Marseille is essential for accessing maps, staying in touch with loved ones, and sharing your adventures.

Here's what you need to know about mobile network coverage, SIM card availability, and internet access:

1. Mobile Network Coverage: Marseille has excellent mobile network coverage, and major service providers such as Orange, SFR, Bouygues Telecom, and Free Mobile operate in the city. You can expect reliable network coverage throughout most areas, including the city center, suburbs, and popular tourist destinations.

2. SIM Card Availability: You can easily purchase a SIM card in Marseille for your unlocked GSM phone. SIM cards are available at mobile network provider stores, electronics stores, and even some convenience stores. Be sure to bring your passport, which is required for SIM card registration.

3. Prepaid SIM Cards: Prepaid SIM cards are affordable for visitors. They offer various data, calling, and texting plans to suit your needs. Depending on how long you'll stay and how much data and minutes you need, you can opt for short-term plans or pay-as-you-go options.

4. Top-up Options: To recharge your prepaid SIM card, you can purchase top-up vouchers at convenience stores, tobacco shops (Tabacs), or online through the mobile network provider's website or mobile app. Top-up vouchers come in different denominations, allowing you to choose the amount that suits your usage.

5. Internet Access: Besides mobile network coverage, Marseille offers several options for internet access. Most hotels, cafes, and restaurants provide free Wi-Fi for their patrons. You can also find internet cafes in the city center where you can access the internet for a small fee. Furthermore, public libraries often offer free internet access to visitors.

It's important to note that while using mobile data or making international calls, roaming charges may apply depending on your home country and mobile network provider. It's recommended to check with your provider regarding international roaming rates and consider using messaging apps or internet calling services to stay connected without incurring additional charges.

10.3 Useful Communication Apps

To enhance your communication capabilities while in Marseille, consider installing the following useful communication apps on your mobile device:

1. Google Translate: Google Translate allows you to translate words, phrases, and sentences between different languages. You can type or speak your query; the app will provide real-time translations. It also offers offline translation for specific languages, which can be handy without an internet connection.

2. Maps and Navigation Apps: Apps like Google, Apple, or Maps. I can help you navigate Marseille's streets, locate points of interest, and find the most efficient routes to your destination. They often provide real-time traffic information, public transportation, and walking directions.

3. Messaging and Voice Calling Apps: Messaging apps like WhatsApp, Telegram, or Facebook Messenger enable you to send text messages, make voice and video calls, and share multimedia files with friends and family. These apps use internet connectivity, so they can be a cost-effective way to stay in touch with loved ones back home or fellow travelers.

4. Local Transportation Apps: Mobile apps can further navigate Marseille's transportation system. The official transportation app, RTM (Régie des Transports Métropolitains), provides real-time information on subway and bus schedules, maps, and service disruptions. Additionally, apps like Uber or Lyft can be used for convenient and reliable ridesharing services.

By utilizing these apps and staying connected with a local SIM card, you'll have the tools and resources to communicate effectively, navigate the city, and access information on the go.

Embrace the Language and Stay Connected

Embracing the local language and understanding the communication options in Marseille will enhance your travel experience and foster meaningful interactions with locals. By using basic French phrases, you'll show respect for the local culture and create memorable connections. Additionally, staying connected through mobile network coverage, obtaining a local SIM card, and utilizing communication apps will ensure you have the information and connectivity you need to make the most of your adventures in France's Mediterranean gem.

CHAPTER 11: TRAVEL TIPS AND ETIQUETTE

In order to have a pleasant and hassle-free trip to Marseille, it is crucial to get acquainted with practical travel advice and the local customs. In this chapter, we will provide you with valuable advice on packing suggestions, weather considerations, and cultural customs. We'll also offer guidance on tipping, greetings, and appropriate behavior in public places. By following these tips, you'll be well-prepared to navigate Marseille and respect the local culture and customs easily.

11.1 Packing Suggestions

When preparing for your trip to Marseille, consider the following packing suggestions to ensure you have everything you need for a comfortable and enjoyable stay:

1. Clothing: Marseille enjoys a Mediterranean climate with hot summers and mild winters. Pack lightweight and breathable clothing for the summer months, including shorts, skirts, t-shirts, and dresses. It's also advisable to bring a light sweater or jacket for cooler evenings. Pack warmer layers such as sweaters, long-sleeved shirts, and a waterproof jacket during the winter. Remember to pack comfortable walking shoes, as Marseille's cobbled streets and hilly neighborhoods are best explored on foot.

2. Weather Considerations: Marseille experiences a lot of sunshine throughout the year. Remember to bring along some sunscreen, sunglasses, and a hat to shield yourself from the harmful effects of the sun. In the summer, bringing a refillable water bottle to stay hydrated is also advisable, as the temperatures can get quite hot.

3. Electrical Adapters: Marseille uses the Europlug Type C and Type E electrical outlets like the rest of France. If your electronic devices have different plug types, pack the appropriate adapters to ensure you can charge your devices.

4. Travel Essentials: Don't forget to pack travel essentials such as your passport, travel documents, travel insurance information, and a copy of your accommodation reservations. Having a small first-aid kit with basic medications, band-aids, and any necessary prescriptions is also a good idea.

5. Language and Communication: Consider bringing a pocket-sized French phrasebook or downloading a language translation app to assist with basic communication. Additionally, having a portable charger for your mobile devices will ensure you stay connected throughout your travels.

11.2 Local Customs and Etiquette

Respecting local customs and observing appropriate behavior is key to positive interaction with the people of Marseille.

Here are some guidelines to help you navigate local customs and etiquette:

1. Greetings: When meeting someone for the first time, greeting them with a handshake and maintaining eye contact is customary. A simple "Bonjour" (hello) or "Bonsoir" (good evening) is appropriate, depending on the time of day. In more casual settings, friends may greet each other with a kiss on each cheek.

2. Politeness and Respect: Politeness is highly valued in French culture. Always say "please" (s'il vous plaît) and "thank you" (merci) when interacting with locals, whether it's in shops, restaurants, or public places. It's also important to address people using formal titles, such as "Madame" for women and "Monsieur" for men unless invited to use first names.

3. Tipping: Tipping is less common in France than in some other countries, as service charges are often included in the bill. However, it is customary to round up the bill or leave a small tip as a gesture of appreciation for exceptional service. If you receive outstanding service or dine at a higher-end establishment, a 5-10% tip is appropriate.

4. Dining Etiquette: When dining out, it's customary to wait to be seated rather than choosing a table yourself. Keep in mind that the French typically take their time during meals, so be prepared for leisurely dining experiences. Keeping your hands on the table but avoiding resting your elbows is polite. Also, avoid starting your meal before everyone at the table has been served.

5. Public Behavior: like any city, Marseille has its own social norms and expectations. Avoid loud or boisterous behavior in public places, especially in quiet neighborhoods or religious sites. Keep noise levels to a minimum on public transportation, and be mindful of others' personal space.

6. Dress Code: While Marseille is a diverse and cosmopolitan city, it's advisable to dress modestly when visiting religious sites or more conservative areas. This means avoiding clothing that is overly revealing or inappropriate. It is advisable to have a scarf or shawl with you, which can come in handy to cover your shoulders if required.

7. Smoking: France has strict regulations on smoking in public places. Smoking is prohibited in enclosed public areas, including restaurants, cafes, and most indoor spaces. Be mindful of designated smoking areas and always ask before lighting up in outdoor seating areas.

Remember, being polite, respectful, and adapting to local customs will help you create positive interactions and leave a lasting impression as a considerate traveler.

11.3 Adapting to Local Culture

Marseille has its own unique culture and way of life. Here are a few additional tips to help you adapt and immerse yourself in the local culture:

1. Embrace the Culinary Scene: Marseille is known for its rich culinary heritage. Try local specialties such as bouillabaisse (a traditional fish stew), pastis (an anise-flavored liquor), and various Provençal dishes. Feel free to ask for recommendations from locals and explore lesser-known areas to uncover hidden culinary treasures.

2. Respect Quiet Hours: In residential areas, observing quiet hours during the afternoon and late at night is customary. This means avoiding excessive noise or loud activities during these times to show consideration for the residents.

3. Explore Local Markets: Marseille's vibrant markets, such as Le Vieux Port and Marché Noailles, offer a glimpse into daily life and provide an opportunity to sample local produce and delicacies. Enjoy the bustling atmosphere, interact with vendors, and appreciate the sights, sounds, and flavors.

4. Embrace the French Art of Slow Living: France is renowned for its emphasis on enjoying simple pleasures. Take the time to savor your meals, appreciate the city's beauty, and engage in leisurely activities like people-watching at a café or strolling along the promenade. Embracing the art of "joie de vivre" will allow you to experience the Marseille way of life fully.

By following these travel tips and etiquette guidelines, you'll be well-prepared to navigate Marseille with confidence and respect for the local culture. Embrace the unique customs, savor the local cuisine, and be open to new experiences. Marseille's rich history, vibrant atmosphere, and warm hospitality await you as you embark on your adventure in France's Mediterranean gem.

CHAPTER 12: MAPS AND ITINERARIES

This chapter will provide valuable maps and sample itineraries to help you navigate Marseille and make the most of your time in this beautiful Mediterranean city. Whether you're a history buff, a nature enthusiast, or a food lover, we have tailored itineraries to suit various interests and durations of stay. So grab your map and explore Marseille's adventure and cultural treasures!

12.1 Map of Marseille

Having a map of Marseille will serve as your guide to the city's top attractions, transportation options, and essential landmarks. It will help you navigate the streets, plan your routes, and maximize your time in Marseille. You can find detailed maps at tourist information centers and hotels or download a digital map on your smartphone for easy access during explorations.

12.2 Sample Itineraries

To help you plan your visit to Marseille, we have created sample itineraries that cater to different interests and durations of stay. Feel free to customize them based on your preferences, but these itineraries will serve as a starting point to help you make the most of your time in Marseille.

Itinerary 1: Marseille Highlights (2 Days)

Day 1:

- Morning:

- Start your day at the Vieux Port, Marseille's iconic old port. Take in the bustling atmosphere and enjoy a leisurely breakfast at one of the waterfront cafes.

- Visit the historic neighborhood of Le Panier, known for its narrow streets, colorful facades, and artistic vibe. Explore the quaint shops, boutiques, and art galleries.

- Make your way to the Cathédrale La Major, a magnificent Romanesque-Byzantine cathedral. Admire its impressive architecture and enjoy panoramic city views from its esplanade.

- Afternoon:

- Head to the MuCEM (Museum of European and Mediterranean Civilizations), a modern architectural masterpiece. Discover the fascinating exhibits of the museum and delve into the rich history and culture of the region.

- Cross the pedestrian bridge to Fort Saint-Jean, next to the MuCEM. Wander through the fort's gardens and enjoy stunning views of the Mediterranean Sea.

- Evening:

- Enjoy a delicious dinner at a traditional Provençal restaurant in the lively neighborhood of Cours Julien.

Indulge in local specialties such as bouillabaisse or ratatouille.

- After dinner, stroll along the Promenade de la Corniche and watch the sunset over the sea. End your day with a drink at a waterfront bar and soak in the vibrant nightlife of Marseille.

Day 2:

- Morning:

- Explore the historic neighborhood of Le Vieux Port and visit the fish market, Marché aux Poissons. Experience the vibrant atmosphere and observe the local fishermen selling their catch of the day.

- Take a boat trip to the Château d'If, an iconic fortress located on the nearby island of Frioul. Explore the historic prison and enjoy panoramic views of Marseille from the island.

- Afternoon:

- Visit the Basilique Notre-Dame de la Garde, Marseille's iconic landmark. To get to the basilica, you can either take a bus or hike up the hill. Once you're there, you'll be able to admire its magnificent architecture as well as the stunning views of the city and the sea.

- Wander through the picturesque neighborhood of Vallon des Auffes, known for its colorful fishing boats and charming waterfront restaurants. Enjoy a leisurely lunch by the sea.

- Evening:

- Immerse yourself in Marseille's lively nightlife by exploring the trendy neighborhood of Cours Estienne d'Orves. Enjoy live music, theater performances, or dine at one of the chic restaurants in the area.

Itinerary 2: Outdoor Adventures and Nature (4 Days)

Day 1:

- Morning:

  - Begin your adventure with a visit to the Calanques National Park. Take a boat tour or hike along the coastal trails to discover the stunning limestone cliffs, hidden coves, and crystal-clear turquoise waters.

- Afternoon:

  - Enjoy a picnic lunch at one of the scenic spots in the Calanques. Take the opportunity to swim, snorkel, or relax on the beach.

- Return to Marseille in the late afternoon and explore the charming neighborhood of Les Goudes. This fishing village offers beautiful coastal walks and seafood restaurants.

Day 2:

- Morning:

- Embark on a hiking excursion in the Massif des Calanques. Select a trail that matches your physical condition and relish the stunning scenery.

- Afternoon:

- Continue your outdoor adventure with a kayaking or paddleboarding experience in the Calanques. Explore hidden caves and secluded beaches while enjoying the beauty of the Mediterranean Sea.

Day 3:

- Morning:

- Explore the Parc Borély, a vast park located near the seafront. You can choose to take a relaxing walk or rent a bike to explore the gardens, lakes, and botanical areas of the park.

- Afternoon:

- Visit the Parc National des Calanques Information Center to learn more about the park's flora, fauna, and conservation efforts. Take part in guided nature walks or educational programs.

Day 4:

- Morning:

- Discover the islands of the Frioul archipelago. Take a boat from Marseille to explore the island of Ratonneau or swim in the pristine waters of the île de Pomègues.

- Afternoon:

- Relax and soak up the sun on the island's beaches.

Enjoy a picnic or try some water activities like snorkeling or paddleboarding.

Itinerary 3: Art and Culture (3 Days)

Day 1:

- Morning:

- Start your day with a visit to the Musée des Beaux-Arts de Marseille. Explore the extensive fine art collection, including works by local artists and renowned European masters.

- Afternoon:

- Visit the Musée d'Histoire de Marseille, located in the Centre Bourse. Immerse yourself in the city's history through interactive exhibits and archaeological artifacts.

Day 2:

- Morning:

- Explore the contemporary art scene at the Friche la Belle de Mai, a former tobacco factory turned cultural center. Discover the galleries, artists' studios, and vibrant street art.

- Afternoon:

- Head to La Friche's rooftop terrace for panoramic views of Marseille. Enjoy a meal at one of the rooftop restaurants or cafes, soaking in the artistic atmosphere.

Day 3:

- Morning:

- Visit the MuCEM (Museum of European and Mediterranean Civilizations) to explore the intersection of art, history, and culture. Discover the museum's exhibitions and attend any special events or temporary exhibits.

- Afternoon:

- Explore the Le Panier neighborhood, known for its artistic spirit. Wander through the narrow streets with colorful street art, boutique galleries, and artisan workshops.

These sample itineraries are designed to provide a starting point for your explorations in Marseille. Feel free to mix and match activities, add your interests, and explore independently. Marseille's vibrant culture, breathtaking landscapes, and rich history will captivate you, regardless of your itinerary.

Remember to refer to your map for directions and consult the local transportation options mentioned in previous chapters to travel to the various attractions and neighborhoods. Enjoy your adventures in Marseille, and may each day be filled with unforgettable experiences and cultural discoveries!

CHAPTER 13: USEFUL CONTACTS

This chapter provides you with essential contact information to ensure a safe and convenient stay in Marseille. When you find yourself in need of help from local tourism offices, your embassy or consulate, or during an emergency, having the right contacts can make a big difference.

Here are the important contact details you should have at your fingertips:

13.1 Local Tourism Offices

When you're exploring a new place, the local tourism office can be an incredibly helpful resource for information and support. They can provide maps, brochures, and recommendations to help you maximize your time in Marseille.

Here are the contact details for the main tourism offices in Marseille:

1. Marseille Tourist Office:

- Address: 11 La Canebière, 13001 Marseille, France

- Phone: +33 (0)4 91 13 89 00

- Website: www.marseille-tourisme.com

2. Office de Tourisme et des Congrès du Pays d'Aubagne et de l'Etoile:

- Address: 1, Cours Barthélemy, 13400 Aubagne, France

- Phone: +33 (0)4 42 03 49 98

- Website: www.tourisme-paysdaubagne.fr

It's advisable to reach out to the tourism offices before your trip to gather information on the latest attractions, events, and any specific guidelines or restrictions that may be in place.

13.2 Embassies and Consulates

If you're a foreign traveler and require assistance from your embassy or consulate during your stay in Marseille, here are the contact details for some of the major diplomatic missions in the city:

1. United States Embassy:

- Address: 2 Avenue Gabriel, 75008 Paris, France

- Phone (emergency): +33 (0)1 43 12 22 22

- Website: fr.usembassy.gov

2. Embassy of the United Kingdom:

- Address: 35 Rue du Faubourg Saint-Honoré, 75008 Paris, France

- Phone (emergency): +33 (0)1 44 51 31 00

- Website: www.gov.uk/world/organisations/british-embassy-paris

3. Embassy of Canada:

- Address: 130 Rue du Faubourg Saint-Honoré, 75008 Paris, France

- Phone (emergency): +33 (0)1 44 43 29 02

- Website: www.canadainternational.gc.ca/france

4. Embassy of Australia:

- Address: 4 Rue Jean Rey, 75015 Paris, France

- Phone (emergency): +33 (0)1 40 59 33 00

- Website: france.embassy.gov.au

Please note that these are just a few examples, and it's important to contact your respective embassy or consulate in Marseille for the most up-to-date and accurate information.

13.3 Emergency Hotlines

It's crucial to be aware of the local emergency hotlines in emergencies. The following numbers will connect you to the appropriate authorities in Marseille:

- Emergency Services (Police, Ambulance, Fire): 112

- Police: 17

- Medical Emergencies (SAMU): 15

- Fire Department (Pompiers): 18

These hotlines are available 24/7, and operators are trained to handle various emergencies. It's recommended to have these numbers saved in your phone and easily accessible in case of any unforeseen circumstances.

13.4 Other Important Contacts

Here are a few additional contact details that may be helpful during your stay in Marseille:

- **Lost or Stolen Credit Cards:** Contact your credit card provider immediately to report the loss or theft. Ensure to note down the customer service number your credit card company provided before your trip.

- **Lost or Stolen Passport:** It is recommended to notify the local police department if your passport is stolen or lost, and then get in touch with your embassy or consulate for help in getting a new one.

- **Medical Assistance:** If you require non-emergency medical assistance during your stay, contact your travel insurance provider for guidance on local healthcare facilities and clinics.

Remember, carrying a physical copy of these important contact numbers is always a good idea in case your electronic devices are lost, stolen, or run out of battery.

Stay Informed and Connected

Access to valuable contacts is essential for a safe and hassle-free travel experience in Marseille. Whether you need information, assistance, or emergency support, these contacts will ensure you have the necessary resources. Stay informed, stay connected, and enjoy your adventure in France's Mediterranean gem with peace of mind.

CHAPTER 14: ADDITIONAL RESOURCES

In this chapter, we provide a list of additional resources that can assist you in planning your trip to Marseille. These resources, including websites, guidebooks, and apps, will offer valuable information, insights, and convenience to enhance your travel experience. Whether you're seeking more in-depth knowledge about Marseille's history, seeking recommendations for local cuisine, or exploring interactive maps, these resources will be valuable companions on your journey.

14.1 Websites

1. Marseille Tourism Official Website (www.marseille-tourisme.com): The official tourism website of Marseille provides comprehensive information on attractions, events, accommodation, and transportation options. You can find detailed itineraries, practical travel tips, and up-to-date information on local festivals and cultural events.

2. Lonely Planet

(www.lonelyplanet.com/france/marseille): Lonely Planet offers detailed travel guides, articles, and recommendations for Marseille. Their website provides insights into the city's attractions, history, culture, and practical information to help you plan your trip.

3. TripAdvisor (www.tripadvisor.com): TripAdvisor is a valuable resource for traveler reviews, ratings, and recommendations for hotels, restaurants, attractions, and activities in Marseille. You can find genuine reviews from fellow travelers, making it easier to make informed decisions.

4. Marseille-Provence Airport Official Website (www.marseille-airport.com): If you're arriving or departing from Marseille-Provence Airport, their official website provides flight information, transportation options, and other services available at the airport.

14.2 Guidebooks

1. "Lonely Planet Provence & the Côte d'Azur" by Lonely Planet: This guidebook covers a broader region, including Marseille, and provides comprehensive information on attractions, accommodations, dining options, and travel tips.

2. "DK Eyewitness Travel Guide: Provence & the Côte d'Azur" by DK Eyewitness: This visually appealing guidebook offers detailed information on Marseille and the surrounding region. It features maps, illustrations, and insider tips to help you explore the area.

3. "Rick Steves Provence & the French Riviera" by Rick Steves: Rick Steves' guidebook provides practical advice, cultural insights, and recommended itineraries for exploring Marseille and the Provence region. It also includes maps, walking tours, and useful tips for travelers.

14.3 Apps

1. Visit Marseille (iOS, Android): The official app of the Marseille Tourist Office provides offline maps, detailed information on attractions, practical travel tips, and event listings. It offers audio guides, walking tours, and recommendations for dining and shopping.

2. Google Maps (iOS, Android): Google Maps is a reliable app for navigation, directions, and finding points of interest in Marseille. It offers real-time traffic updates, public transportation directions, and the ability to save maps offline without an internet connection.

3. Marseille Travel Guide and Offline City Map (iOS, Android): This app provides a comprehensive travel guide for Marseille, including information on attractions, restaurants, nightlife, and shopping. It also offers an offline

city map, making it accessible even without an internet connection.

4. Marseille Metro and Tram Map (iOS, Android): This app provides the Marseille metro and tram map, including information on lines, stations, and schedules. It helps you navigate the city's public transportation system conveniently.

These additional resources will complement the information in this guidebook, giving you access to more detailed insights, user reviews, and interactive features. You will receive assistance in planning your itinerary, finding the best places to eat, uncovering hidden gems, and navigating Marseille with ease.

CHAPTER 15: CONCLUSION

As we end this travel guidebook, "Travel Guide Marseille: Your Passport to Adventure and Culture," I want to express my sincere appreciation for joining me on this journey through France's Mediterranean gem. Throughout the chapters, we have explored the captivating city of Marseille, delving into its history, cultural treasures, adventure opportunities, and vibrant culinary scene. This guidebook has provided valuable insights, practical information, and inspiration to plan an unforgettable trip to Marseille.

Marseille is a city that truly has it all. From its rich history as a major Mediterranean port to its stunning natural landscapes, there is something for every traveler to enjoy. Whether you're a history enthusiast eager to explore ancient landmarks, an outdoor adventurer seeking thrilling experiences in the Calanques National Park, or a food lover ready to indulge in Provençal cuisine, Marseille offers many opportunities to satisfy your interests and create lasting memories.

Throughout this guidebook, we have covered the essentials you need to know before your trip. We started with an introduction to Marseille, highlighting its significance as a cultural hub and a gateway to the French Mediterranean. We then provided general information about the destination, including its location, climate, time zone, currency, and entry requirements.

In subsequent chapters, we guided you through various aspects of planning your trip to Marseille. We covered transportation options to reach the city, recommended accommodations for every budget, and outlined the top attractions and activities that should be noticed. We delved into the vibrant dining scene, introduced you to local delicacies, and highlighted entertainment options to experience Marseille's nightlife and cultural events.

We also provided:

- Practical tips on shopping for souvenirs.
- Ensuring your safety and health during your stay.
- Navigating local transportation.

- Communicating in the local language.

- Adhering to local customs and etiquette.

In addition, we offered maps, itineraries, and useful contacts to assist you in exploring Marseille with ease and confidence.

To complement this guidebook, we recommended further resources such as websites, guidebooks, and apps that can enhance your travel planning and provide additional information and insights about Marseille.

As you embark on your adventure in Marseille, I encourage you to embrace the spirit of discovery and immerse yourself in the city's vibrant culture, history, and natural beauty. Take the time to wander through its charming streets, interact with the friendly locals, and savor the flavors of the Provençal cuisine. Allow yourself to be captivated by the breathtaking views from the Calanques, immerse yourself in the art and history of the city's museums, and find your hidden gems within its diverse neighborhoods.

While this guidebook has provided a comprehensive overview of Marseille, it is important to remember that travel is about personal experiences and creating unique memories. Allow yourself to deviate from the suggested itineraries, follow your interests, and discover the unexpected. Marseille has a way of captivating its visitors with its warm hospitality, rich cultural heritage, and boundless opportunities for adventure.

Finally, I would like to express my gratitude to the city of Marseille for its incredible history, culture, and hospitality. The spirit of Marseille is palpable, and I am confident it will leave a lasting impression on your heart.

Thank you for choosing "Travel Guide Marseille: Your Passport to Adventure and Culture" as your companion in discovering this Mediterranean gem. May your journey be filled with unforgettable moments, new friendships, and a deep appreciation for the wonders Marseille offers.

Bon voyage!

Printed in Great Britain
by Amazon